花 木 兰 的 故 事
——中国古代女英雄

The Legend of Mu Lan
A Heroine of Ancient China

姜 巍 根 兴 编绘

Written and Illustrated by
Jiang, Wei and Gen Xing

胜利出版社
Victory Press

花木兰自幼跟着父亲习武健身，练就一身好武艺，刀枪棍棒，样样皆通，骑马射箭，百发百中。

Since she was young, her father taught her to fight with swords, spears and poles. She also learned to ride horseback and shoot with a bow and arrow. She was good in all different types of martial arts.

这日，花木兰的父亲接到皇帝派人送来的军书，讲边境敌人来犯，形势非常紧张，要父亲再赴战场。

One day a messenger appeared at the door. He had an order from the emperor for Mu Lan's father, General Hua. Enemies from the north were invading China and the situation was serious. Mu Lan's father was ordered to return to the front lines to fight.

花木兰越发不安了,她进屋说:"二老不用发愁,木兰愿替父应征。"父摇头说:"朝廷有明文规定,不要女子!行不通,行不通!"

Mu Lan entered their room and said, "Father, Mother, don't worry. I can fight for father." General Hua shook his head as he replied, "The law says females are not allowed to join the army. It is impossible."

次日清晨，一个英姿飒爽的青年军人站在父母面前；"二老请看，女儿能上前线吗？"弟弟花木礼惊叫道："原来是姐姐女扮男装啊！"

The next morning a sharply dressed young soldier stood before General and Mrs. Hua, and asked, "Father, Mother, now can I join the battle ranks?"
"Oh! It's you Mu Lan, dressed as a soldier!" Mu Li, Mu Lan's younger brother cried out in surprise.

这日，花木兰率兵马扫
北来到中国现在的承德东北的
摩天岭，只见悬崖峭壁，敌兵屯
居山上，从下面休想攻得上去。

One day Mu Lan led troops to
Mount Mo Tien (present day
Cheng De City in He Bei Prov-
ince in China). The enemy had
already occupied the steep cliff
and were camping on top. It
seemed almost impossible to at-
tack the enemy from the base of
the mountain.

花木兰回到大帐,想起自己从军已十几年了,十分怀念爹娘和小弟,怀念乡亲们,恨不得一脚踏平摩天岭,早日班师回朝。

Mu Lan returned to her tent and thought. She had been fighting for over ten years. She missed her parents, younger brother and other relatives. She wished she could flatten Mount Mo Tien in one step and lead her troops home.

花木兰解甲归里，还了女儿身。当同伴们知道这位英俊赫赫有名的花将军，原来是一位亭亭玉立的女子时，无不惊讶万分。花木兰替父从军和荣立战功的事迹就这样广泛流传开来了。

Mu Lan returned to her farming village and handed over her military uniform to the soldiers accompanying her. When they saw she was really a female, their surprise was boundless. From this time on, the story of Mu Lan spread throughout China.